From Bitter to Blessed

Companion Guide

Lesley Carney

This companion guide is designed to accompany *From Bitter to Blessed* and is intended for personal use or group study.

Scripture quotations are taken from the Holy Bible, New International Version® NIV®.
Copyright © 1973, 1978, 1984, 2011 by Biblica, Inc.™
Used by permission. All rights reserved worldwide.

ISBN: 9798245801551

Disclaimer:

This guide is not intended to provide professional counseling or medical advice but is offered as a faith-based resource for personal reflection and growth.

Author's Note

If you're holding this guide, there's a reason you're here.

It may be a burden you've been carrying.
Unresolved questions.
Or simply you feel it's time for a change.

Wherever you are, you're not alone.

Through this companion guide, I invite you to go beyond reading my story and begin walking your own journey, applying biblical truth, reflecting honestly, and taking meaningful steps toward healing.

I urge you to take the next step. You are not alone.

Table of Contents

Starting the Journey

This guide is designed to walk with you through the journey from brokenness to healing, one step at a time.

In addition to *From Bitter to Blessed* and this companion guide, you will want to have your Bible nearby. Each session is rooted in Scripture and is meant to help you connect God's truth to your own story.

As you move through each session, you'll have opportunities to reflect, respond, and take meaningful steps forward. This isn't about rushing or getting through pages. It's about being honest, taking your time, and allowing God to meet you right where you are.

Let this be personal. Let it be real.

And remember, you are not walking this journey alone.

Where Am I on the Journey?

Place a check beside where you believe you are right now. You may see yourself in more than one place, and that's okay.

- ☐ **Standing at the Beginning**
  I know something needs to change, but I'm not sure where to begin.

- ☐ **Carrying the Baggage**
  What I've been holding onto feels heavy and hard to ignore.

- ☐ **Searching for Direction**
  I'm asking questions and trying to understand.

- ☐ **Taking Steps Forward**
  I'm beginning to process and move toward healing.

- ☐ **Learning to Trust the Path**
  I'm choosing to trust God, even without all the answers.

- ☐ **Walking in Freedom**
  I can see growth, healing, and forward movements in my life.

Setting Your Direction

Every journey has direction, not because we have everything figured out, but because we are willing to take the next step forward.

My prayer for you is:

You will begin to see your story with greater clarity and that you will release what has been weighing on your heart.

You will experience healing in places you may have thought would always hurt and most of all…

That you will come to trust God with every part of your journey, even the parts that still feel uncertain. You don't have to have all the answers now…

You just need a willingness to move forward.

My Direction for This Journey

Take a moment to think about what you desire from this journey. In light of where you are right now, what do you hope will change?

Write your thoughts below.

What do I want from this journey?

_____

_____

_____

_____

What am I ready to release or let go of?

_____

_____

_____

_____

What do I want God to do in my life through this journey?

_____

_____

_____

_____

SESSION 1

The Ground Shifts

Reading for this Session
Chapter 1 – The Bump
Chapter 2 – The Legacy

Session Overview

Every journey begins somewhere—often in moments we did not expect.

In this session, we begin exploring how unexpected circumstances can shape the path ahead and how God is often working quietly within those moments long before we recognize His purpose.

As you move through this session, consider how the unexpected turns in your own life may have shaped your journey.

Insights from the Journey

When Lesley first learned that her teenage son was going to become a father, the news came as a shock. Like many parents in that situation, she was faced with a mixture of concern, uncertainty, and questions about what the future might hold.

Yet within that unexpected moment, something meaningful began to grow, the love between a grandmother and her granddaughter.

Over time, that relationship developed through visits, traditions, and everyday moments that quietly built a lasting bond. What seemed like ordinary parts of family life were actually shaping a relationship that would become deeply significant.

Looking back, these early chapters remind us that some of the most meaningful parts of our story begin in moments we never planned. What first feels like a disruption may later reveal itself as the beginning of a journey God is gently unfolding.

Scripture for the Journey

Proverbs 16:9 (NIV)

"In their hearts humans plan their course, but the Lord establishes their steps."

Pause and Reflect

Think about a time when life took a direction you did not expect. How did that experience shape the path your life eventually followed?

Psalm 139:16 (NIV)

"All the days ordained for me were written in your book before one of them came to be."

Pause and Reflect

How does knowing that God sees your entire story from beginning to end change the way you view uncertain moments in your life?

Jeremiah 29:11 (NIV)

"For I know the plans I have for you," declares the Lord, "plans to prosper you and not to harm you, plans to give you hope and a future."

Pause and Reflect

Where in your life do you find it most difficult to trust that God is still working for your good?

Faith in the Journey

Mary — Trusting God with an Unexpected Path

When the angel appeared to Mary, her life changed instantly. She was young, engaged to be married, and suddenly faced an unexpected future that would reshape everything she thought her life would be.

Mary did not fully understand what the road ahead would hold. Yet she chose to trust God even when the future seemed uncertain.

Like Mary, we sometimes find ourselves stepping into circumstances we never planned. The path may feel unfamiliar, but God is still present in the unfolding story.

Scripture Reference: Luke 1:26–38 (NIV)

Heart Reflection

Unexpected moments often shape our lives in ways we cannot immediately see.

1. Think about a moment in your life when something happened that you never saw coming. How did that experience influence the direction of your journey?

_____

_____

2. Relationships often shape the deepest parts of our hearts. What relationships in your life have had the greatest influence on who you are today?

_____

_____

3. Looking back on your story so far, where can you see moments when God may have been quietly guiding your path—even if you did not recognize it at the time?

_____

_____

Truth to Carry Forward

Life does not always unfold according to the plans we carefully make. Yet even when the path ahead looks different than we expected, God is still present in the unfolding story.

What truth from this session reminds you that God is still guiding your journey, even when the path changes?

_____

_____

_____

Your Next Step

Unexpected changes often require us to release the plans we once held tightly.

Take time this week to reflect on the unexpected turns in your life. Ask God to help you see how He may have been quietly guiding your story—even in moments that once felt uncertain or difficult.

My Next Step This Week

Write one step you will take this week as you continue your journey toward healing.

_____

_____

_____

Prayer Pause

Take a quiet moment to talk with God about the unexpected turns in your life. You may want to thank Him for the ways He has guided your journey so far, or ask Him to help you trust Him with the parts of your story you still do not fully understand.

Write your prayer to God below.

_____

_____

SESSION 2

The Avalanche

Reading for this Session

Chapter 3 – The Last Year

Session Overview

Some moments in life change everything.

In this session, we explore how quickly circumstances can
shift and how a single event can alter the course of a
relationship, a family, and a heart.

As you move through this session, consider how unexpected
moments of loss or heartbreak have shaped your own
journey.

Insights from the Journey

In Chapter 3, the relationship Lesley had carefully built with
her granddaughter over many years begins to unravel in
ways she never anticipated.

The chapter reflects on what would ultimately become the
final year of their relationship before everything changed.
Small shifts in communication and subtle changes in
behavior gradually created distance that could not yet be
fully explained.
At first, these moments seemed like temporary tensions,

things families often work through. But as time passed, the distance grew more noticeable and the uncertainty more painful.

Then, in a moment that felt sudden and overwhelming, the relationship came to an abrupt and devastating end.

What had once been a cherished and active connection was suddenly gone, leaving Lesley stunned and searching for answers.

Many of us experience moments like this in life, moments when something we deeply value is suddenly taken away. These "avalanche" moments can leave us feeling confused, hurt, and unsure how to move forward.

Scripture for the Journey

Psalm 34:18 (NIV)
"The Lord is close to the brokenhearted and saves those who are crushed in spirit."

Pause and Reflect

When heartbreak enters our lives, it can feel as though we are facing the pain alone.

How does this verse reshape the way you think about God's presence in moments of deep hurt?

Isaiah 41:10 (NIV)

"So do not fear, for I am with you; do not be dismayed, for I am your God."

Pause and Reflect

When life suddenly changes and the future feels uncertain, fear often takes hold.

What fears tend to surface when your world feels unstable?

_____

_____

_____

Job 1:20–21 (NIV)

"The Lord gave and the Lord has taken away; may the name of the Lord be praised."

Pause and Reflect

Job experienced devastating loss and struggled to understand why it had happened.

When painful events occur in your life, what questions do you find yourself asking God?

_____

_____

_____

Faith in the Journey

Job — Holding on to God During Loss

Job's life changed dramatically in a single day. In a series of devastating events, he lost his possessions, his livelihood, and his children.

The loss was overwhelming. Job did not understand why these tragedies had happened, yet he continued to bring his pain before God.

Like Job, we sometimes find ourselves facing circumstances that leave us searching for answers. In those moments, faith may feel fragile, but God remains present even when we do not understand His purposes.

Scripture Reference: Job 1:13–22 **(NIV)**

Heart Reflection

Painful moments often raise questions that are difficult to answer.

1. Have you ever experienced a moment when everything seemed to change suddenly? What emotions surfaced during that time?

---

2. When a relationship or situation you value begins to unravel, what thoughts or fears tend to rise in your heart?

_____

_____

3. In seasons of heartbreak, it can be difficult to see where God is at work. What helps you hold on to faith during those times?

_____

_____

Truth to Carry Forward

Moments of heartbreak can leave us feeling lost and uncertain. Yet even when everything around us seems to collapse, God is still present with us in our pain.

What truth from this session reminds you that God remains near even in the hardest moments of your journey?

_____

_____

_____

Your Next Step

When painful experiences occur, our first instinct may be to search for explanations or try to make sense of what happened.

This week, bring one painful experience in your life honestly before God. Instead of trying to solve or explain it, simply acknowledge the hurt and place it in His hands.

My Next Step This Week

Write one step you will take this week as you continue your journey toward healing.

Prayer Pause

Take a quiet moment to talk with God about the pain or confusion you may be carrying. You may want to tell Him honestly how this experience has affected your heart and ask Him to help you trust that He is still present with you.

Write your prayer to God below.

SESSION 3

The Aftermath

Reading for this Session
Chapter 4 – Facing the Rubble of Grief
Chapter 5 – The Cracks Begin to Show
Chapter 6 – Embracing Vulnerability

Session Overview

After a devastating moment, life rarely returns to normal quickly.

This session explores what it means to live in the aftermath of loss and how grief often reveals the deeper places in our hearts that need healing.

As you move through this session, consider how seasons of grief or disappointment have shaped your own journey and what those experiences may be revealing about your heart.

Insights from the Journey

In the chapters that follow the painful break in the relationship, Lesley finds herself facing the emotional aftermath of what has happened.

The shock of the moment has passed, but the weight of the loss begins to settle in. Questions linger. Memories resurface.

Everyday moments that once brought joy now carry a quiet ache.

Grief has a way of revealing the deeper places in our hearts. As Lesley continues moving through life, the emotional cracks created by the loss begin to show in unexpected ways.

Eventually, she begins to recognize that healing cannot happen while pain remains hidden. The journey forward requires honesty about what the heart is carrying and the courage to become vulnerable with both God and others.

Scripture for the Journey

Psalm 13:1–2 (NIV)

"How long, Lord? Will you forget me forever? How long will you hide your face from me?"

Pause and Reflect

David expressed his grief and confusion openly before God.

Have you ever found yourself asking God questions like these during a painful season?

Psalm 62:8 (NIV)

"Trust in him at all times, you people; pour out your hearts to him, for God is our refuge."

Pause and Reflect

This verse invites us to bring our honest emotions before God.

What feelings have you been carrying that you may need to bring openly to Him?

_____

_____

_____

2 Corinthians 12:9 (NIV)

"My grace is sufficient for you, for my power is made perfect in weakness."

Pause and Reflect

Sometimes our weakest moments are where God begins doing His deepest work.

Where do you feel most vulnerable in your life right now?

_____

_____

_____

Faith in the Journey

David — Bringing Grief Honestly Before God

Throughout the Psalms, David expressed his deepest emotions to God—grief, confusion, anger, and fear. Rather than hiding those feelings, he poured them out honestly in prayer.

David's words remind us that faith does not require us to pretend we are strong. God invites us to come before Him with our true emotions and trust Him to meet us in our pain.

Like David, we can bring our broken hearts to God and know that He hears every cry.

Scripture Reference: Psalm 13 (NIV)

Heart Reflection

Grief often reveals emotions we may not have expected to face.

1. When you experience loss or disappointment, do you tend to process your emotions openly or keep them hidden from others?

---

2. Vulnerability can feel uncomfortable, yet it often opens the door to healing. What fears make it difficult for you to share your pain with others?

_____

_____

3. What might it look like for you to allow God—and perhaps someone you trust—to see the places in your life where you feel broken?

_____

_____

Truth to Carry Forward

Healing often begins when we stop pretending that everything is fine and allow ourselves to face the truth of what we are feeling.

What truth from this session reminds you that God welcomes honesty and vulnerability in your relationship with Him?

_____

_____

_____

Your Next Step

Grief often tempts us to hide our pain or carry it alone.

This week, consider taking a step toward honesty about what you are feeling. That may mean spending quiet time with God in prayer, writing honestly about your emotions, or sharing your experience with someone you trust.

My Next Step This Week

Write one step you will take this week as you continue your journey toward healing.

_____

_____

_____

Prayer Pause

Take a quiet moment to speak honestly with God about the emotions you may be carrying. You may want to ask Him for the courage to face your pain and the strength to trust Him with the healing process.

Write your prayer to God below.

_____

_____

SESSION 4

The Crossroads

Reading for this Session
Chapter 7 – The Battle with Bitterness
Chapter 8 – Wrestling with God

Session Overview

Pain does not simply disappear with time. Instead, it often forces us to confront deeper questions about our hearts, our faith, and how we will respond to what has happened.

In this session, we explore the internal struggle that can arise when wounds remain unresolved and how the choices we make in those moments can shape the direction of our spiritual journey.

Insights from the Journey

As time passes, the pain Lesley carries begins to shift from raw grief to a deeper internal struggle. Questions about the situation continue to surface, and with those questions come emotions that are difficult to navigate. Bitterness can quietly take root when wounds remain unresolved. What begins as hurt can slowly grow into resentment, frustration, or anger. During this season, Lesley finds herself wrestling with difficult questions about faith and the circumstances she is facing. Why did this happen? Why would God allow such a painful loss? And how does a person continue trusting God when the answers do not come easily?

These chapters reveal a turning point in the journey. The struggle is no longer only about what happened, it becomes about how the heart will respond moving forward.

Scripture for the Journey

Hebrews 12:15 (NIV)

"See to it that no bitter root grows up to cause trouble and defile many."

Pause and Reflect

Bitterness can grow quietly when pain is left unresolved.

Are there areas of your life where resentment may be taking root in your heart?

_____

_____

_____

Psalm 139:23–24 (NIV)

"Search me, God, and know my heart; test me and know my anxious thoughts. See if there is any offensive way in me, and lead me in the way everlasting."

Pause and Reflect

When you invite God to search your heart, it requires honesty and openness.

Are there areas in your life where you may be resisting what God wants to reveal or change?

Isaiah 26:3 (NIV)

"You will keep in perfect peace those whose minds are steadfast, because they trust in you."

Pause and Reflect

When our focus shifts toward trusting God, peace begins to follow.
What would it look like for you to fix your thoughts on God rather than your circumstances?

Faith in the Journey

Jacob — Wrestling with God

Jacob's encounter with God was not calm or easy. In fact, the encounter was marked by struggle. Throughout the night, Jacob wrestled, refusing to let go until he received a blessing.

By morning, Jacob walked away changed.

Sometimes faith is not expressed through quiet certainty but through honest struggle. Like Jacob, we may wrestle with God as we try to understand the circumstances we are facing.

Yet even in the struggle, God is working to shape our hearts and lead us toward transformation.

Scripture Reference: Genesis 32:22–31 (NIV)

Heart Reflection

Seasons of pain often force us to confront emotions we may not want to face.

1. When you have been deeply hurt, what emotions tend to surface first: anger, sadness, confusion, or something else?

_____

_____

2. Bitterness can quietly grow when wounds remain unresolved. What helps you recognize when resentment may be taking root in your heart?

_____

_____

3. Wrestling with God can feel uncomfortable, yet it can also deepen our faith. What questions have you brought, or need to bring, honestly before God?

_____

_____

Truth to Carry Forward

Struggling with God does not mean faith has failed. Sometimes the very act of wrestling with difficult questions is part of the journey toward deeper trust.

What truth from this session reminds you that God welcomes your honest questions and struggles?

_____

_____

_____

Your Next Step

When pain leads to difficult questions, we may feel tempted to withdraw from God rather than bring our struggles to Him.

This week, consider taking an honest step toward God by bringing one question or frustration directly before Him in prayer. Rather than hiding your struggle, invite God into it.

My Next Step This Week

Write one step you will take this week as you continue your journey toward healing.

_____

_____

_____

Prayer Pause

Take a quiet moment to talk honestly with God about the questions or emotions that may be stirring in your heart. If you feel anger, confusion, or frustration, bring those feelings before Him and ask Him to help you find peace and clarity.

Write your prayer to God below.

_____

_____

SESSION 5

A New Perspective

Reading for this Session
Chapter 9 – The Lies, The Truth, and the Armor
Chapter 10 – Healing Isn't Instant

Session Overview

Painful experiences can shape the way we see ourselves, others, and even God. Over time, those experiences can create beliefs that quietly influence our thoughts and emotions.

In this session, we explore how God begins to replace harmful beliefs with truth and how healing often unfolds gradually as we learn to see our story through a different lens.

Insights from the Journey

As Lesley continues processing the pain surrounding the broken relationship with her granddaughter, she begins to recognize that the struggle is no longer only about what happened, it is also about the thoughts and beliefs forming in her heart.

Unresolved questions and lingering hurt can give way to internal narratives that distort the truth. Thoughts like *"What did I do wrong?" "Was I not enough?" "Will this pain ever go away?"* begin to take hold.

In Chapter 9, Lesley starts confronting those internal messages, realizing how destructive they can become if left unchallenged. Instead of allowing those lies to shape her identity, she begins replacing them with the truth found in God's Word.

But even as truth takes root, healing does not happen overnight.

Chapter 10 reminds us that healing is often a slow and ongoing process, as God patiently restores the wounded places of the heart. In this stage of the journey, Lesley begins to see that while pain may linger for a time, God is still working beneath the surface—bringing restoration and a renewed perspective.

Scripture for the Journey

John 8:31–32 (NIV)

"Then you will know the truth, and the truth will set you free."

Pause and Reflect

Sometimes the beliefs we carry about ourselves, or our circumstances are shaped by pain rather than truth.

What thoughts or assumptions have you formed during difficult seasons that may need to be examined in light of God's truth?

_____

_____

_____

Romans 12:2 (NIV)

"Do not conform to the pattern of this world but be transformed by the renewing of your mind."

Pause and Reflect

Transformation often begins when our thinking begins to change.

What might it look like for you to allow God to reshape the way you think about your story?

_____

_____

_____

Psalm 147:3 (NIV)

"He heals the brokenhearted and binds up their wounds."

Pause and Reflect

Healing is not something we create ourselves—it is something God works within us.

Where do you see signs that God may already be working to restore parts of your heart?

Faith in the Journey

Joseph — When God Rewrites the Story

Joseph's life included betrayal, rejection, and years of suffering. His own brothers sold him into slavery, and many of the events that followed seemed unfair and painful.

Yet over time, Joseph came to recognize that God had been at work even through those difficult circumstances.

Instead of allowing bitterness to define his story, Joseph eventually saw how God had used those experiences to accomplish something greater than he could have imagined.

Like Joseph, we may not immediately understand how God is working through painful seasons. But over time, He can begin to reshape our story in ways that reveal His faithfulness and purpose.

Scripture Reference: Genesis 50:19–21 (NIV)

Heart Reflection

Changing the way we see our story often begins by identifying the thoughts we have been carrying.

1. Have you ever noticed negative beliefs about yourself or your situation forming after a painful experience? What were those thoughts?

---

2. What truths from Scripture help counter those beliefs and remind you of how God sees you?

---

3. Healing rarely happens quickly. How can you give yourself grace as God continues working in your heart over time?

Truth to Carry Forward

Painful experiences may shape our story, but they do not define our identity. God's truth has the power to reshape the way we see ourselves and the circumstances we face.

What truth from this session reminds you that God is still working in your story?

_____

_____

_____

Your Next Step

Healing often begins when we intentionally replace harmful thoughts with truth.

This week, identify one negative belief or lie that has surfaced in your mind during difficult seasons. Then search Scripture for a truth that directly counters that belief.

Write that truth somewhere you will see it throughout the week.

My Next Step This Week

Write one step you will take this week as you continue your journey toward healing.

_____

_____

_____

Prayer Pause

Take a quiet moment to ask God to help you recognize any harmful beliefs that may have taken root in your heart. Invite Him to replace those thoughts with His truth and continue His work of healing within you.

Write your prayer to God below.

_____

_____

SESSION 6

Moving Forward

Reading for this Session
Chapter 11 – Forgiveness: The Path to Healing
Chapter 12 – Trusting God with the Future

Session Overview

Healing often reaches its turning point when we release the burdens we have been carrying and choose to trust God with what we cannot control.

In this final session, we explore the role of forgiveness in the healing process and what it means to move forward in faith even when life has not unfolded the way we expected.

Insights from the Journey

As Lesley continues walking through the pain of losing the relationship with her granddaughter, she begins to realize that holding on to the hurt is only prolonging the weight she carries.

Forgiveness does not erase what happened, nor does it deny the depth of the loss. Instead, it becomes a deliberate choice to release the grip that pain and resentment can hold over the heart.

In Chapter 11, Lesley confronts the difficult but freeing reality that forgiveness is not primarily about the other person, it is about allowing God to heal the wounds that bitterness cannot fix.

Chapter 12 brings the journey to a place of surrender. While the circumstances of the relationship remain unresolved, Lesley chooses to trust God with the future of what she cannot control.

The journey from bitterness to blessing is not defined by restored circumstances but by a transformed heart. Through forgiveness and renewed trust in God, Lesley discovers the freedom that comes when we release our story into God's hands.

Scripture for the Journey

Colossians 3:13 (NIV)
"Forgive as the Lord forgave you."

Pause and Reflect

Forgiveness is often one of the most difficult steps in the healing process.

What makes forgiveness challenging in situations where you have been deeply hurt?

_____

_____

_____

Matthew 11:28–30 (NIV)

"Come to me, all you who are weary and burdened, and I will give you rest."

Pause and Reflect

Carrying unresolved pain can become exhausting over time.

What burdens might God be inviting you to release to Him today?

_____

_____

_____

Proverbs 3:5–6 (NIV)

"Trust in the Lord with all your heart and lean not on your own understanding."

Pause and Reflect

Trusting God often requires surrendering our need to understand everything that has happened.

What part of your story feels hardest to entrust to God right now?

_____

_____

_____

Faith in the Journey

Jesus — The Ultimate Example of Forgiveness

While suffering on the cross, Jesus spoke words that revealed the depth of His mercy:

"Father, forgive them, for they do not know what they are doing." *(Luke 23:34)* **(NIV)**

Even during unimaginable pain, Jesus chose forgiveness.

His example reminds us that forgiveness is not dependent on whether someone deserves it or whether circumstances change. Instead, forgiveness becomes a reflection of the grace we ourselves have received from God.

When we choose forgiveness, we are not excusing the hurt that occurred—we are entrusting justice and healing to God.

Heart Reflection

Forgiveness and trust often require intentional decisions of the heart.

1. Is there someone or something you have struggled to forgive? What emotions surface when you think about releasing that hurt?

_____

_____

2. Forgiveness is sometimes misunderstood as forgetting or excusing the past. How might forgiveness instead become a step toward freedom for your own heart?

_____

_____

3. As you consider the future, what fears or uncertainties do you need to entrust to God?

_____

_____

Truth to Carry Forward

Freedom often begins when we release the burdens we were never meant to carry alone. Forgiveness and trust open the door for God to continue His work of healing within our hearts.

What truth from this session encourages you to move forward in faith?

_____

_____

_____

Your Next Step

Moving forward often begins with a simple but intentional decision.

This week, spend time asking God to help you release any lingering resentment, bitterness, or fear you may still be carrying. Consider writing down the specific burden you want to place in His hands and pray over that decision.

My Next Step This Week

Write one step you will take this week as you continue your journey toward healing.

_____

_____

_____

Prayer Pause

Take a quiet moment to speak with God about the areas of your life where forgiveness or trust may still feel difficult. Ask Him to give you the strength to release what you have been carrying and the faith to trust Him with what lies ahead.

Write your prayer to God below.

_____

_____

Looking Back on the Journey

You've taken steps on this journey, some that may have felt small, and others that may have felt significant.

Before moving forward, take a moment to pause and reflect on where you are now.

At the beginning of this study, you identified where you were on your journey. Now that you have completed these sessions, return to that page and look at it again.

Has anything shifted?

You may find that you are no longer in the same place. Or you may realize you are still working through some of the same areas, but with a new awareness or perspective.

Both are part of the journey.

Take a few moments to revisit "Where Am I on the Journey?" and mark where you see yourself now.

On the back of this page is where you can reflect on what has changed.

What has shifted in my thinking, my heart, or my perspective?

_____

_____

_____

What truth has impacted me the most during this journey?

_____

_____

_____

Where do I see growth in my life even if it feels small?

_____

_____

_____

What is God continuing to work on in me?

_____

_____

_____

Truths I'm Carrying with Me

Throughout this journey, you've identified truths that matter. Truths that speak to your life, your healing, and your relationship with God.

These are the truths you don't want to forget.

Return to them often. Let them remind you of what God has shown you and what you are continuing to learn.

Truths I'm Carrying with Me

My Next Steps on the Journey

Growth happens when we take what we've learned and begin to live it out.

These are the steps you've chosen to take, whether small or significant, as you continue your journey.

Revisit these often. Continue building them as you grow.

My Next Steps

_____

_____

_____

_____

_____

_____

_____

_____

_____

Leading the Journey

This section is for those who are leading a group through this study, whether in a church, small group, or informal gathering.

Leading others through this journey is not about having all the answers.

It's about creating a space where honesty is welcomed, stories can be shared, and God's truth can be explored together.

You are there to walk alongside others as they move through their own journey.

Overview of the Journey

This study is designed to be completed over six sessions. Each session builds on the previous one, guiding participants through both the emotional and spiritual progression of the journey.

1. **The Ground Shifts**

2. **The Avalanche**

3. **The Aftermath**

4. **The Crossroads**

5. **A New Perspective**

6. **Moving Forward**

Each session includes reflection, Scripture, discussion, and personal application to help participants connect Lesley's story to their own lives.

Preparing for Each Session

Before meeting with your group:

- Read the assigned chapters

- Review the session content

- Spend time in prayer

- Be ready to guide

Suggested Format

This is a flexible guide. Adjust the timing as needed based on your group size and the time you have available.

- **Welcome & Opening (5–10 minutes)**
  Casual connection and opening prayer

- **Session Reflection (10–15 minutes)**
  Briefly revisit the session theme

- **Discussion & Sharing (30–40 minutes)**
  Walk through key questions together

- **Personal Application (10–15 minutes)**
  Allow time for reflection and writing

- **Closing Prayer (5 minutes)**

About the Author

Lesley Carney is a speaker, author, and former educator with over 25 years of experience working with students, teachers, and families.

Through her own journey of pain, healing, and transformation, she has developed a passion for helping women move beyond what has hurt them and walk forward in faith.

Lesley is the author of *From Bitter to Blessed*, where she shares her personal story of healing and the role her faith played in that process.

Her heart is to encourage women to trust God in every season and to continue growing, healing, and moving forward in their own journey.

Made in the USA
Coppell, TX
15 April 2026

75717670R00036